somnieeee
by Kristin Peterson

somnieeee ©2019 by **Kristin Peterson**. Published in the United States by Vegetarian Alcoholic Press. Not one part of this work may be reproduced without expressed written consent from the author. For more information, please contact vegalpress@gmail.com

Cover art by **Amanda Huff**

for Bethany, Annie, + Ben

my heart, the hole, is the front cover
    underneath is the worn pail where water once dripped, now rusts the rim
        the joust and gesture of shared pleasure   a tipped card
where the illustrations of my relative but not related self is printed
      my heart, the hole, began as the front cover
is now   the sodden bound child

the inner-thigh-most hoax
    of my elusive patriotic nap
the juniper'd night rest   in a pocket out-turned
  my miserable numbering of days
the reliable need to need everything until a furtive collapse
        cancelling plans before they're made   cashing in everyone's
told you sos   the consistently scratched itch   now a stain of red on the
sheets

she wears turtlenecks like she's god and she invented them

your home is a kaleidoscope
of everything you've done
everything he's done
and what you kept along the way

it is lovely

we are in no wilmington motel
we are beneath no wilmington motel - we are pinked in shorts
we are not breaking a sweat - our panties do not face the street
we go home and we work it all out - she stays up late on stage
and i sleep inside me - we get itch cream inside the rose garden
we wear the nights down with red velvet curtains and monstrous lounges
we thrift outside pagan pride - we scheme to gain nothing - we scheme
- for a cup - of jasmine - for a cup - of amethyst
- we are so heavy with purchased meaning
- we avoid each other's eyes inside the heavyliddedness
of an occidental rock concert - we bless each other's hearts under the soaked
umbrella - under the rain - under the stares of such southern folk
the southernmost folk - we are using our caucasian tape to hold the world up
- we are shoeless under this sudden southern pour
we are shoeless - skimming stones up blacktopped hills up escape routes
we are learning what it really means to bless another's heart
we are taxied home - we are swift door shut and locked - we are talked out
runnels dried under hardwood floor and sleeping bags - we are in/between
two stately buildings - like cowboys - facing east and facing west
poised to draw a biker's fleet against a biker's fleet - but the cascades
frighten every fleet away - we fotograph our knees - shelly buys our drinks
i am dripping in the misogyny of the place - the fuchsia on billiards
the waxed abdominals on plush screens - the faerie lights glyphing over
a scene: a blue-most fountain - an empty concrete dance floor - a triplet
of young lesbians chittering at the gaffs of the skirtless and sweatered stranger
a triplet of young lesbians alert at the emphatic new-found woman
pleasured to be heeled - unfettered in wig purchases - unspun in identity
convinced not one of us will forget her - unforgotten by rulebook - by law
and i promise - i bless this promise - that i will do it all - this forgetting business
i will forget the disrespect to balance - i will dispel the swift occultation of the
becoming a woman - and ask you questions and questions
that will pressure you to find the right answer - the answer where it turns out
everyone waits outside

    i wait outside - contemplate the possibility of my throwing my cig in between the car and the curb - so as not to disrespect the volvo in front of me - i dawdle
 - we are remotely rooftop lounge - we are remotely almost there -
    we are remotely sensing the
server's disdain - we are ransacking the unbussed table
- we are ordering each course one at a time - one after the other - it is all in steps
this woman blessed me with plastic bags for my wet clothes - i don't have wet clothes
- i might have wet clothes - it is taking us three years to circle up the parking ramp we see logos at the top - we are motown at the top
- it is taking us three years to find a parking spot nearer to the bottom
- we are home-chatting on an oddly non-entry porch - we meet a for sale sign
- she tells us a new story - a new story everyday - she tells us to get ourselves to l.a.
- i tell myself i will never be able to remember everything she said - she said so much
- all looking at us so curiously - we find remedy in coffee and pie and forgetting the menu the moment the bartender finishes listing and listing the menu and listing the menu
- a fibbing libra - an incomprehensible disinterest
- all at the same time grabbing at us - taking us - kneading us so well - do you know what she means? - we leave sweating from smoker's lung capacity - hip dancing disaster
- a despairing cuckold pays our tab - he asks me why his young wife left him for korea
- for malaysia - for anywhere but here - I say
i am not her

how miserly the mist can be
when it fails to cover me

i realized i had been drinking her water this whole time
but not before she put it as far out of my reach

as possible
and i spent the whole dinner considering making light of it

and neglecting the glass that was mine

i scan through my photos of memories from the past year
i note the way my old apartment looked before the lover moved in
i note how it was after
i see that made bed
i see that unmade bed
i notice i stopped taking pictures of him sleeping
i whip through these photos and take the time to delete the ones i won't need to see again
and i think to myself, the book was better

i'll blend you up
blend you up so fast
you'll burn

most of us don't live our lives in aether
would you open the doors of a mind
that knocks in aether would you wait
in line with a mouth that winces aether
would you hold a spat with the busted
knuckle of a saint, doused in aether? would
you hold my bottoms, creep, while i jump in the
aether would you tell your friends about the croatian
pussy you licked into aether would you save me from
the aether when i go out every night looking for aether
would you call my mom when i am lost in aether would
you take me to the beach where there is none and no more
and left to ask where is that aether? why isn't there any aether!

you scarcely know (or is it the opposite?) whether it is too late, until it is too late
or, wait, was it that the odds are in the numbers
the count
when you learn the game
I mean, can we just agree to share.

can we rest easy knowing we think the same
that you took so long that it lasted longer
or was it at first thought - wait, what was i even saying?

it'
s nice to b
e teas
ed (in a harsh world) by
a kind
man

you'
ve tricked
em

& god is only as good as his worst criminal

ligated one-night-stands jump above   the memes of love
the motion of quotient butter-ups   the results of divisions
of the skinless mash-ups   the release of finders keepers
the grown terra cotta potted summer   bell peppered porch
the porch with soaked couch cushions   without shared space
the numbered button-down   before your lace measurements
before your brother remembered your name   when he forgot his

the whole crew's allergic to ginger
yet ginger - it's all we have to whet

today i am my own nadir
i don't feel like
this is a hole i can jump out of
alone

mostly because i am stubborn
and likely because i need that thrill
i have learned the most impossible things

but why
    did i have to hold off
on learning how to climb
a rope

it is the cherry picked lips
    admitting they don't know how to drive stick shift
and they don't intend to learn

last night

she told the story quickly and seemingly by rote
like she had written this disclaimer a hundred times
the disclaimer gets to the point, leaves nothing to the imagination
it is brief and clean

she told it with her eyes looking at the dull dip in the ceiling
her eyes transfixed so she could focus on the script
get it over with
brief the listener

so they could definitely move on
and when she was done
he looked at her like he wanted more

and she kept talking
she kept talking until her eyes did the crying
and her mouth, her teeth, her tongue, her roof of her mouth did the rowing
the hard work

the tale telling

and she is still talking now

my shoes are unmuddied
at the thought of you

i glance at you and your face is the cat's arched back
with ridges between thoughts as you run them past me
and then i notice the sensation of touching myself
while you watch as you speak and i listen and
it is the double sided touch that i don't get when you touch me
or when i touch you
the thought of zippering my pants and the zipper feels itself rumble
without choosing and then it's unzipped again
and i thumb my phone around in my purse and i feel the twirl on my thigh
through the toughened cloth and i glance
i see that i've been using my phone's calculator to call you all this time
and this must be why you've never picked up
why you were surprised to see me, to run into me
on the way home from your new lover's home

writing is too lonely an occupation
when the words themselves are sad, too,
and you grow needy for a hug, a whistle,
a broken bottle that fizzes into your cup
and you wake up the next day having only
thought about writing

the fear of having children is really
the fear of sending them to bed supperless

would choose watching a video of a slug leaving the frame over sex

whatever comfort there is
when she's there to look at you with brown eyes
whatever comfort there is when she's there
whatever comfort when she's there to look

i am the sores on your forehead
i am the song heard around the world
i am the exit wound
i am the archdiocese
i am the poisonous berry
i am the spread of the apple tree
i am yellowed with my tea parties
i am amplified out here!
i am the algae in my personal pond
i am the reflexive verb
i am in love with the new sea
i am probably so far off in asia!
i am the deal to strike,
i am ripe with this manifested

pickling your birth certificate
has the west yet heard it was me?
i entered through the rockies
here to claim in my diary who i meet
sitting fine in my pink belly
and the domestication of the bronco

i am simplified indeed!
won't you come and visit me?
on your savage honey
and its god nuances

take it or leave.
dining destiny.

your voice is a reminder that i can hear
that i am not just a breathless body rising and falling
with the air pressure in the room, from the vent, in the room
that i am not a spore multiplying in lonely microscopy
that i am not a pair of ears without anything to hear

i don't require three locks on my bathroom stall
but sure as hell don't mind it

he says, "i'm not fun,
don't say that.
but I had fun.
so, thanks."

i say, "i hate that
you think that."

he says, "me too."

if only i could bookmark what you say   if only i could tell you your self
is my weekly prayer   if i could wave you down if i saw you in real life
if i could wave you down until you looked at me looking at you and this is the
hello   a solemn   intense touch of life lived and time on time
this is what it is   a moment   it is happening
a gentle wrinkling wave   you tug with your own claw
beneath my face   the highlight on your arms
a bouncing ray through ripples   and here we are
two possible strangers and the
scavenger birds up ahead   licking their lips at us
knowing that you taste like sugar   and i like butter
scoping out our coming together
wishing for a bite of their own lick-reddened lips,
ourselves
diverging   converging
diverging   converging
diverging

i want him to know my nail beds, how they are made everyday
 & i want him to know which foot i choose to step with first, which foot
gets to choose my way and when my knee clicks on the third step
     and how i still do not know how little conditioner my hair needs
i want him to know my name, my truest name   i want him to know before me
which color mug i would want with how much coffee i want at what time i want

it is the least we can do
to wait

for the moment our lovers finesse
the act of
treating us well

where does one find a set of sterling silver cocktail sticks
when you know the person you want to gift will never use them?

the protestants are the punks of the zodiac!

we are our own pieta
my head draped beyond your forearm
and your gaze through me

i lay here
through each pause

tell them, i was allowed to rest then
with my body the curve in the upper surface
of your lap

and god checks the devil's facebook
to see if he's happy, to see if he's doing well
to see him

matches in a new box - the boring bell drums - the booms between booms altering a new prince in the hinted bold benigh - benigh - benigh - know a loss at its loss - ponds for the rich - the new children - the new needed needy - marbled milk beneath each pronoun - each thinkpiece - each thinkpiece written to justify - each thinkpiece written to justify one insecurity at once - the 5 paragraph lean-in by white mama on a tapestry'd bottom over a staircase covered in polyester wool - the cursed quilts condemned to the tupperware tub far into the corner of a basement only the 10 year old in desperate need of privacy will find - the vast foray into self intimacy - the primary decision before dinner call to celebrate its child's body - to learn why his knees click going down the steps, but not when going up them - justify these knees - new rhombus-ness in the guts of a childhood - a childhood's just a pocket of waiting, for the next phase - to be aware that you are just preparing for the next phase - a cruel limbo before the word limbo is defined - always wondering if you're left out - always aware that the majority of the call sheet is kept from you - always the last to know what's up - the last to be asked what you're thinking - treated as the first and the forethought - treated as malware of your surroundings - kept in the dark - for lack of a better phrase, but how would you know where better phrases are? - jail is a musical set - sex is a second act character arch essential - murder is a no-no, no-no - people marry people - women make pies from berries - women make curd from yodeling goats - women make women so quickly - men are warriors - little animals are harmless - the news is the breakfast soundtrack - tired is sleep - soda is celebration - the simplistic memes are curious new concepts - grandma is grandpa's - the christmas morning is for meals on wheels - church is for reading the map of jerusalem for an hour - temperance is sitting less close to the television - temperance is the dollar worth a dollar - the toothache is the fallen tooth - the fear of the dark is insurmountable - the bed is not to be shared with you - the bed is not to be shared with you - the bed is not to be shared with you - the equation is a sample of frustration - you are not to be trusted with dangerous things

"believe me you," she says, "when i know, i'll shout"
     and the notebooks were stacked by rank   the usurped secret
but a vehicle overturned   until
porridge & pies enveloped   in the hydraulic'd love for a word well-chosen
mustard oculars
predetermined license to gnaw on bones
     a private chat room in the penny-drop whisper-fountain
many windows open all at once   a rolled sunshine of away messages
what is life but the determined looks and the frame of skeletal fence posts bowed
over a firm pillow?   what is life but the discussion of ourselves
beside ourselves   i want to behold you
but barely can behold myself

i can't bare to behold myself   when i want to just
plainly   the buttercream frosting on a woodman's cake plainly beholds you
beside ourselves, we discuss ourselves   and what seems to be living
over a firm pillow   becomes a yonder truth of shirked postings on fences
so skeletal   so framing on the determined looks from those who don't know
our lives

what seems to be living while we're away, while we roll ourselves in sunshine
while our many windows remain open   and we won't need to gnaw anymore
allowed to look through any ocular refracting beams of coarsed yellow
          our words so frightfully chosen over waterpump over strengthened
over conditioned into the rank of written words
waiting for the shout of our sisters   who will shout, of course, when they can

the days i feel tired of myself
of the voice neither soft nor sharp   but calibrated by myself for myself
when i feel tired of my vanity -- my patina'd list making, the me of superiority
my general outlook against deserts against the ill against the dull
it is the day(s) i feel tired of myself that now
are the doormen for the days i
walk out of the bath --- twice fresh
---- ready

i wrote with one hand, "how are you?"
and the other hand said, "bored"
so i asked that hand, "what do you want to do about it?!"
it said, "breathe"
and then i asked it if it'd go on a date with me to the park
where we could, i don't know, read or walk or talk about things
and it said, "sure" so i went home and hung up stained glass stickies
to the tops of the windows
and now i write while the green crosses my face

manners are the expression of value
          of letting the other person know you know
they exist and that you exist too in this world
where a 'thank you' is really the 'i see you'
and the 'please' is the 'I know a war is about us
and here's my lotioned palm holding a wet flag
on top of the olive branch and laurel wreath
at your doorstep, at your feet'

also: manners make an ass out of you and me

i am the gold whisper
that has nothing to say

sushi sushi su
shi sushi sushi sushi
sushi sushi su

sat below oneself - beside mellow muster
the pantomimed umber - the picture perfect apology
the sun kissed closeness - massaged further away
the fierce goodbye - under the bridge

our eyes - the madcaps in the cracks - in the sidewalk
looking up the skirts of the many-few people that pass
their knees pickled by the pressure of foot poaching
our own eyes cuckolded by each other - the immoderate mess
of desiring ourselves to be our own stockpile - the annexed me
the posturer - now the pirate of the selfsame self
each earmarked identifier now the feckless giveaway
that we've amassed a number of moments in a sieve with one big hole

i am taking notes
breathlessly   and without measurable words
but i am noting her thoughts and her margins between a number of wonders
and a number of worries   her face is now half in shadow
when she leaves the cafe

the consistent and opposite urges to
dissect and to
connect

i will be alarming i will
be an alarm a ditto-ing
i will be   an arm on
the whom i love   i am
the repeated me i am the
coda with the skin on
i am the disc of rest i am
the alarming wist of love
i am the love   i am my own
will to live   with a quoted
repeat of my heart on you

you witness these stairs that carry your steps
assigned cushions for the rocking of small bones
you wander your logs from room to yard
and at the moment you search for a crutch
a strata of mourners walk by on commute from home
to comfort to home to comfort to home to comfort to home
you witness the seams and lodes made through moments alone
these old and new mourners riding the long backed goodbye
counting the layers of tolerant numbers, pretty and neat,
and now your dinnertime reversed from two to none, easily
remembering what you will have never done

actually, we are a broken
glass   it's a collection
under another collection
  and we duet together
in separate rooms
a fract of a tune

actually, it's my
rediscovery   and you
aren't even there
actually, it's my dismissal
actually,
i am the poorly chopped
     vibration   in actuality,
i am but beside you
     actually, i am grown
on the side of a felon
(this felon is not you)
        actually, i am let go

actually, i am a good deed
suspected of cheating
actually, i am not even here
actually, you did this all on your own

our lives are stained with pure
light   our laughter and our
warmth of darling admiration
mutual and deep

i almost forget there are people
out there   even at arm's length
that want to bite my neck out
that want to fence me out
that want to box up all my beauty
and belongings until i die
until i have no will to claim it all

and here you are
the both of you have burned love into me
and it is more than tangible
it is more present than any physical
worldly
worrisome thing

and life is a big broom
brushing all its dust and crumb
past our faces and we sit,
we marvel at its motion

and when glass is there
and when this collection of shattered objects
swift with the dust and crumb
we sit back, we note to ourselves in our hushed corner booth
"it is hard not to see this glass as glitter
when we are together
this glass
is glitter
when you're near"

so i am laying down in the doorway
my cheek cold on the ground
waiting for someone to notice me
for someone to see that i am in two rooms at once
that i'm not standing up

i ate my own cancer
with someone else's mouth
and it sits in someone else's stomach
as i carry on with my day

i am in this body hoping for someone to notice
that i am trapped   hoping they calmly, squarely
ask me to blink twice if i can hear them
to blink three times if i need help
and to stop blinking
altogether if i want to be left alone

you keep offering everything you have
with the follow-up: not that you need it

landlines still exist
for the sheer joy of it

i'd want the pain to come in   single file
taking turns
politely   without shoving
i'd want the chasms to be filled with orbs of air
instead of the impulse to be reckoned with
pleasantly or not   i'd want to be left in peace
but the great lonesomeness has a loud head
and a belt for whipping

edit: i want to be left in peace, full stop

the debt collector called
he sounded like how a newspaper looks
and i wish i could pay him so he'd fold up
and drop in a puddle

jokes on you   the incremental change of the soul
incremental change after years of not changing at all
is it really a competition whose body works the best
and why haven't i joined in the parade of bodies yet
why haven't i competed in my section yet
if it really is a competition of whose body works best
i can win even though i know i can't but i could
i very well could if i tried but i never even tried did i

she is a pineapple   she is helpless until she's not yours anymore
helpless until she's nobody's anymore
the cat moves to the naked chair
but does the same waiting for me
to look at it, to look at it, to look at it and wait
and it meows once i've looked at it enough
as if to ask where i was on my way to before i became distracted by the pet
the pet that doesn't know it is a pet

i am a pineapple before pineapples knew what they meant to people
before people made them mean something to other people
before pineapples were a way of saying, i have and you do not
before pineapples were a way of saying, i am in a body that is better than yours
and my wealth follows me whether i have good posture or not

i knock on her door and i hold a pineapple in my arms
ready to show her that i brought it for her and i've also brought her mail
but the mail was already so close, and the pineapple was close enough too

much to say about the mister whispers
the terrible oblong harper's bazaar listicles
much to say about your groped legs
in midwest warmed-thawed hot tubs
therein the much to says are lost
wherein the much to says are kin
and you are not who you thought you'd be
after the years of making your growth to-do's
now dones

each day -- the truest steeplechase over
juxtaposed nothings -- card delays and missed receipts
the family reposes -- and the flash catches each one's eyes
your glibness distastes -- the internet fades
and you fall behind -- each project delayed
the footing you had -- now a crawl
to a finish line that more-than-likely is unowned
and does not exist

pick-an-ocean:
cry cry cry cry cry cry cry cry & cry cry cry cry
until   everyone is swimming   unaware of themselves
and yr ashamed you opened your eyes

i am talking about you now, the you who knew to shy from me
you who knew

i text my brother pictures of plants
to hear back two weeks later
that it was a linden tree i saw
and thought was lovely
luminous
mine

i am a talisman! i am a charm with a face! in a room where people put me! and i go missing! they think they've misplaced me! but i just got bored! wanted to get up and DO things! i am a talisman with legs! i am forgotten after three months!

a love so mondo
it is coda ditto coda

it is the space here where there are one thousand silences
each countable   each inventoried
each silence misplaced in the wrong cupboard
it is here in this space where the doorways guard each room from the others
the color spectrum is forbidden from using the milk   or the butter
the sinus of this home is coated with never-used blankets
a habit of stocking up
on the least needed goods
a habit of inviting guests that will never visit
the room tone is dulled and constant
we are not aware of it any more
and we continue to live together inside the devil's reared head
begging for a shorter life span
but grinning when our housemates pass by
and look our way

some one or more people expired in my apartment building this week
and all i know about them is that whomever is responsible for them
decided to board up their door with green plywood in a green so loud
earlier in the days i joked that a tenant was sloshing fish sauce and
spilling it across the 2nd floor carpets and i now realize that you can describe
anything better if you do not already know the source or its name
and now i know the scent of personhood decay is similar to the fish markets
on the docks where men yell fine code at each other for long learned skills
and those in the market   for fresh and familiar seafood
listen on without the decoder
they expect these fish mongers to address them in their english after they've
finished up with this english and then the folk go home to make a meal most likely
satisfying most likely warm
this is all to say i hope the one or more people that expired and are now boarded
up inside
(do you think they left the body or bodies in there? no, they wouldn't do that?)
i hope the person was not the lovely lady that planted the peppers
and carefully monitored the other plants in the yard and caught me on many
occasions
smoking the guilty cigarette that turned into a habitual cigarette at the greened
picnic bench
with a young man, be it ben or not ben

i hope it is not her because if she caught me every time out there, logic would say
she was out there   every day   making sure
our shared garden was clean and growing
this is all to say i will be sitting out at the picnic table soon around 5pm hoping to
catch her
catching me

have you seen bundled rope fly in the air
and drop with its clonk   dull yet loud
see, other bundles fall in the same way
loudly impacting the ground and themselves
wailing a short song sung for anyone close enough
to call 9-1-1 in unison and wait until the fire truck comes first
and then the ambulance

wishing everyone you see "good luck!"
and meaning it and meaning it and meaning it
shaking each syllable into the shared air
not to deem the future as inevitably dark, ominous
but to point at your fellows and say there is "good luck!"
and meaning it and meaning it and meaning it

the reckless abandon of the woman
who adds mascara to her funeral attire

i whisper an asymmetrical hello to myself the moment i wake up
the rest of the day is crooked and it won't straighten no matter how many times
i adjust myself

"i am at the
top of the eiffel
tower
i am going to jump

                you hate
                    me
                    and if you don't catch
                    me
                    you don't love me," he says

                    just one second before he does,
                    indeed, jump, and i have no idea.
                    i get how many floors down
                    and

                                      everyone but him is
                                      screaming.

you're never fully dressed without some spite

we are all just mirrors looking at ourselves
hoping a mirror is a phonograph
hoping what we sound like is just hearsay

whenever she speaks
it is a quote i say to myself
in the shower   even before
it reaches the right heat
and the water becomes a lyric
before it falls in the tub

spider
dermatongue
the inside of
bottom courage
tired boys
the mazekeep
moreso outside
the tinderbox
versus truth
cold spider misery
but you don't read

maybe the next time
but it's never
ordained
of mysterious
yourself down
to pity you enough

this monster spider
a daredevil timepiece
an extract of faceless
a child now its only

a muse in its own
a triad
until the next day
anymore
being better

okay
do unto yourself
give yourself
give yourself nothing

& grow old in agony

we occupy ourselves
you deserve every
to shatter
before it's built,

in the bottom bowls
jessolution
the chosen ones bullied
sheet paper
of mustard
himself

time is an issue uproar
a must-read list
you don't read &

you open a cheerio's bag
preventable
the clutz of quartzmen
self-failure
don't you look

a time keeper
a clear constant stone
humanity, a bare chested
adult, a notebook

shape
of the most miserable
until the next day
until you won't feel
than you are now

apparently i can't be
the chaste criticism
that terrible beating, give
but the dense misery

so widely with matterless
wince of distress you have
to rust
borne,

of spider beeps
in a system of jeans
tuesday men
a marriage mead
inside the home
of calendar
spider misery
of reasons to be upset
life is your vacation

it'll spill out everywhere
only predetermined
the grasp
a breakfast of letting
for the nearest person
to clean it up

a desperate stripper
a ripped earth
nevermind
now underwater

in its own cellar
under the covers
until it's not a day
any better
apparently i am not

apparently i am
you choose for others
yourself a horrible life
you wish on others

& regardless musings
you deserve everything
to break
or brewed

he takes my post in the palm of his crust
and pulverizes my knuckles from 5 miles away
he takes this innocuous sharing of pursuits,
of cute meme food video sharing into a tug
where at each end is the most miserable
at each end is the tug of who thinks about whom more

it's like i returned a haunted blanket to a mini mart
they gave me cash back, and i thought it was that
but still i think about that blanket after it didn't keep me warm at all
but it left my feet sweaty, the cold that slapped on the palms of my toes
the irk like spanking a wet, defrosted ravioli, the cheese popping out

how violated i feel that i can't do anything to undo it
i can't break into his apartment and unwire his computer
i can't shave his fingers off in his sleep, i can't even tell him to stop
because telling him to stop is telling him he can respond
his clicks on my posts are clicked to show he still monitors me
and wants me to know how monitored i am

i was quoted on a friend's wall today and the first like was his
another insertion. another insertion of his shard self into my life
a life he was sharding inside for years until i heard one word and left
and he wants me to know how much he knows i am there
drunk with thorough frequenting, stumbling past my door
a door he thinks is still my door, but it isn't anymore
and maybe he knows that if he were better at haunting
if he were better at patronizing my whereabouts
and maybe he is better at it, but this is not working
clicking on my post on someone else's wall is not my door
and i know this, but he never gets to know it
i hope it isn't working, this new neo internet sharding of his

when you've broken your back
crouching like a monster   desperately begging for a laugh
or a glance or a knee-jerk sinew of love & affection
the moment before you could have used a back the most
in an embrace   over a cafe table   saying goodbye
to your first friend

you swallow the mint in the middle   your throat is the whisper in the mill
at midnight   with no one and you race to get home
to spend your evening with characters on the screen   unlike you
but at least they aren't you   but at least they are someone
but at least you don't have to be alone alone
high hopes the rest of the rustic road   the moniker'd lusting rope
the humorous last joke   the forever nope
the buttoned beloved holiday no one gives thanks at
we are swallowing   grasping   thawing out

we are swallowing   grasping   thawing out
turn it on full blast   run the way to the top of the hill
where there is nothing but ragged ruck and matter where there is only you, raw
and you cannot swallow anything but the ache you caused yourself
at least you can sleep now   now that you've done it
now that you've clip crawled your own way instead of just taking note
watching the crones with split nails come down and beg for your shoulder
they whisper with white foul breath that first moves down then straight through
your ear canal you listened, you nodded - it made sense but you must grasp, you must tundra
you must swallow the burn yourself and then defrost   thaw out from this all

this mellow mild this mellow mild taste   this need to categorize the calendar
by which man i was with this mellow, mild need to take a man and call him mine
and i get to say when.   and when when is when i begin to swallow, grasp, and thaw
the stand up comedian that fucked me unsatisfied   the nepotist,
the negative werepoet that said i didn't know what i wanted when of course
i just want everything   the want to not be me   the caustic shoulder
the tinder boxed rub of the knife on sandpaper the whatever blood
the no blood   the no blood   of no blood
the little stitch on the button rod of bottoms   the need to be held
the need to listen to someone but me   the bouncing into the seat next to any-body
with a vacant seat   the need to be needed

the last yellow card in a stack of yellow cards   that replaced the stack of white flags
many years ago and yet i still am not fully declawed   defrosted   thawed
but isn't it truly wild that so wild that   you keep me from the busting hearts
the magnificent ways   the exclusion outrights
the mustard bits the southerners the range of marijuana coniferous refrains
the hotel officer the keys given to the wrong room the mistaken bellhop the daisy chain

the chain of fathers refusing to bad mouth their fathers
the chain of daughters not understanding the identity   not knowing who to blame
who to exalt   not understanding that we are all the worst in this pen pot
and since the enemies are enemies, they are anxious for more
for more   for more   for more

catch me from the wad   catch me i am swallowing myself
catch me i am swallowing the perfumed ferret of man
catch me i am the ferret perfumed into a dazed wretched man

the wretched men i am suddenly vacant for

what does it mean to swallow   what does it mean to rend the hallows of one's throat
toward the inside, the belly, the bowel   and what do we do once we have swallowed?
does it mean something if we swallow?   what if i were to swallow you?
would you swallow me? would you swallow me only if i swallowed you first?
who is going to be the brave one?
who is going to draw first?

measure this - the self - the need - the horrendous call
pouted bluffs - opened pride - a blushed descent
mere meniscus - irate lobe - must muster
a note from self to self - the raised hand
called on by no one

i didn't know house stuffing could be so beautiful
not house stuffing, what's the word
what's the word for it, it all everything having a word now
we can't just say a word and hope it's a name
house stuffing, you know, the pink bed curtains that bloom out
and fully and there's a sparkle too, did you know that?
there are white, chalky sparkles and lightly glass sparkles
and i get a long look at it knowing that the next time
(if there's a next time) i see it will be at a dismantling
or an accidental hole in the wall meeting so i keep staring
but nothing moves, nothing changes and i move on

the beat rubs along my ribs
making this satisfying, hollow sound of a tide
ripping down a staircase
and i hear my name in each step, each impact
every other soiled rag flying out on its way down
some say you don't have to live your pain
i say there's no other way

it's not a relief to find out
it wasn't your fault at all
all along
at all

www.ingramcontent.com/pod-product-compliance
Lightning Source LLC
Chambersburg PA
CBHW030236100526
44584CB00015BB/1524